Pass the B1 English Test (Speaking and Listening)

An Essential Guide to British Citizenship/Indefinite Leave to Remain

(The British Citizen Series)

Orders: Please contact Gardners Books LTD, 1 Whittle Dr, Eastbourne, BN23 6QH

You can also order through Amazon.co.uk under ISBN 978-1911259084

ISBN: 978-1911259084

First published in 2017 by Courtney Harvey

Copyright © 2017 Courtney Harvey

All rights reserved. Apart from any permitted use under UK copyright law, no part of this publication may be reproduced or transmitted in any form or by any means, electronic or mechanical, including photocopying, recording, or any information, storage or retrieval system, without permission in writing from the publisher or under licence from the Copyright Licensing Agency Limited. Further details of such licenses (for reprographic reproduction) may be obtained from the Copyright Licensing Agency Ltd, Saffron House, 6-10 Kirby Street, London EC1N 8TS.

Printed and bound by CPI Group (UK) Ltd, Croydon, CR0 4YY

Disclaimer

Every effort has been made to ensure that the information contained within this guide is accurate at the time of publication. The publisher is not responsible for anyone failing any part of any selection process as a result of the information contained within this guide. The publisher cannot accept any responsibility for any errors or omissions within this guide, however caused. No responsibility for loss or damage occasioned by any person acting, or refraining from action, as a result of the material in this publication can be accepted by the publisher.

The information within this guide does not represent the views of any third party service or organisation.

Contents

Your Assessment	15
Preparing for the B1 Tests	25
Exam Language	33
Practice Tests	53
Answers to Practice Tests	105
Final Thoughts	127

Introduction

Introduction

INTRODUCTION TO YOUR GUIDE

Hello, and welcome to your guide, **Pass the B1 Speaking and Listening Test.** If you are reading this, then the chances are you've decided to become a British citizen. This is a brave and exciting choice, which will have fantastic benefits for you. However, it's also time consuming and expensive. The application process is long and arduous. Luckily, this guide is here to help!

As the third book in our *British Citizen Series*, this guide will provide you with a complete breakdown of the B1 Speaking and Listening test. Since 2010, there have been many changes to the UK citizenship laws. So, this book contains the most up to date information for the tests.

The English language speaking and listening test will form an essential part of the process of becoming a naturalised British citizen, or a permanent resident. This test is used in conjunction with the Life in the UK test, where both results will count towards your final assessment. As part of your application for British citizenship, you'll need to provide the Home Office with both sets of results.

In this book, we'll be taking you through the process of passing the B1 Speaking and Listening test.

HOW TO USE THIS BOOK

This book has been written to help you understand how to pass the speaking and listening English language tests. In order to do this, we'll run through both sets of tests, to help you decide which one is the best option for you. Following this, we'll give you advice on preparation, revision and perfecting your language technique, to ensure that you pass the test.

Throughout this book, we've provided you with a number of practice questions, to help you track your progress and recap on what you've learnt. The questions in this guide are extremely similar to what you will encounter in the real assessment, so make sure that by the end of the guide, you are comfortable answering them.

In order to use this book in the most effective manner, we advise that you take notes as you progress. Once you are finished with the content, you can then use these notes in your revision.

This book will cover all 6 learning levels. We'll start with A1 – beginner's level, and then move on to A2 all the way through to C2, which is the most advanced level.

Now, let's move onto learning some key info about the assessment.

ABOUT THE TEST

There are a total of two speaking and listening tests which are currently accepted by the UK Home Office for British citizenship. **Please note:** you only need to pass one of these tests.

These tests are:

- The Trinity GESE Grade 5 Exam;
- The IELTS Life Skills Test.

Both of these tests are run under different formats, but each of them is designed to assess whether the candidate meets the Common European Framework reference (CEFR) standards of English.

The CEFR was created as a guide by the Council of Europe, and is used by the examiners to judge your English skills. The CEFR guidelines are used almost universally, as a way of assessing candidates. The IELTS Life Skills test and the Trinity GESE Grade 5 test both use different tasks to assess users. However, both tests require Independent Users to fulfil the expectations laid out by CEFR.

When taking the assessment, always make sure that you are sitting the test at a Secure English Language Test (SELT) Centre. This is the only centre from which test results will be accepted.

Candidates can choose which test they would prefer to take. If you wish to become a British citizen, or are applying for indefinite leave to remain, then you will need to take the B1 Speaking and Listening test at CEFR B1 level. If you are taking this test, then you will be known as an 'Independent User'. Independent users must prove that they have the necessary skills to deal with key topics of conversation (such as travelling) and other fundamental elements of life in the UK.

Introduction

Please note that if you are from a majority English speaking country, or have achieved a degree which was taught in English, then you won't need to take the assessment.

HOW ARE THE TESTS MARKED?

At each learning level, the tests will assess your speaking, listening, reading and writing skills. If you are applying for citizenship or settlement, then you will only be required to demonstrate your speaking and listening skills.

The B1 test is some way off the required standard for C2 Advanced Users, and therefore it will reassure you to know that it's not too difficult. During your examination, the examiner will cross-check your language skills against a checklist in front of them, to see how closely it matches.

The examiner will also be looking at other qualities, such as the pronunciation of your words and how clearly you speak, the quality of your physical interaction, and how well you understand what they are saying to you.

HOW CAN I IMPRESS THE EXAMINER?

In order to impress the examiner, you will need to show them that you can meet the requirements expected of a B1 Independent User.

The requirements are measured on the following:

- The fluency of your speech;
- The quality of your English interaction;
- The accuracy of your speech;
- Your range of vocab;
- Your pronunciation.

When taking the assessment, you will be expected to talk with the examiner, in simple terms about familiar/everyday scenarios and situations. For example, conversing with someone whilst travelling, asking for directions or ordering a meal.

The assessor will not expect you to talk at the same level as someone who has lived in the UK for their entire life, nor will you be required to speak for long periods of time or about extremely complex subjects. You'll need to show the examiner that you are able to interact to a sufficient level in English, by speaking clearly and accurately, and showing a good range of vocabulary.

INTERACTING WITH THE EXAMINER

When taking your assessment, you won't just be judged on your level of speech, but how well you interact as a whole. So, simply repeating responses to the examiner will not gain you a high mark. You will need to go out of your way to try and interact with them, making comments, agreeing, nodding, shaking your head or asking them extra questions.

On some occasions, you may be asked to sit the test along with another test-taker, who you will need to converse with. The examiner will then judge you based on how well you interact with that person.

Always remember that while you are not being judged on your personality, it's best to be as open and chatty as possible for this assessment. While you might well be able to speak in complex terms about certain subjects, controversial views will not help your case, and could result in you scoring poorly. You should do your best to put your personality across, but don't be overbearing.

One of the best and most basic pieces of preparation advice that we can give you is to practise your speech beforehand. This is especially true if you are someone who often pauses/stops whilst speaking, or struggles to think of things to say. If this is the case, it will be evident in the exam, and you will lose marks. That being said, the examiner will expect you to think for a moment or two before responding. This is normal practice, especially if speaking slowly, clearly and pronouncing each word helps you to demonstrate your language ability.

While you won't be judged based on how well you pronounce certain words or your accent, it's essential that the examiner can understand what you are saying.

VOCABULARY SKILLS

As mentioned, during the assessment you will need to show that you are able to use a wide range of vocabulary. This means being able to use words and phrases from common scenarios and situations. It's important to remember that if you don't understand a particular expression, you are allowed to ask the examiner to clarify or expand on what was said.

While you should try to avoid this where possible, asking for the occasional bit of help won't damage your chances of success. It's far better to ask for clarification, and then give a clear, in-depth and precise answer; than to give an answer that is lacking these qualities. When you do reply to the examiner, it's also best to try and do so in proper English.

While studying for the assessment, or living in the country, there is a good chance you will have picked up certain slang terms. Don't use these. Try and be as formal as possible, without seeming unnatural. Also, being polite is very important.

LISTENING SKILLS

Listening is a core part of the assessment. You'll need to show that you can listen and then respond to lines of conversation, and questions from the assessor. The better you can respond to exactly what is being asked of you, the better your listening skills will be judged.

During the IELTS Life Skills test, there is a chance that you will be required to listen to recordings, and then complete a listening exercise, testing your ability to remember what you have just heard. Therefore, your ability to listen and take in information needs to be at a high level.

THE B1 TESTS

As mentioned earlier in this chapter, there are two types of B1 assessment:

- The Trinity GESE Grade 5 Exam;

- The IELTS Life Skills Test.

You can choose which of the above tests you wish to take. Let's take a look at the two tests in a bit more detail.

CHAPTER 1
Your Assessment

ABOUT THE B1 TESTS

In order to gain your qualification, you will have a choice between two assessments: *The Trinity GESE Grade 5 Test*, or the *IELTS B1 Life Skills Test*.

Both assessments are designed to examine how well you can deal with everyday situations that you'll encounter in an English-speaking country. There is no limit to how many times you can take each test again (if you fail), although you will need to pay for re-takes.

As we have mentioned, the tests will examine your ability to navigate everyday situations that you'll encounter in an English-speaking country.

This includes subjects such as:

- Buying items from a shop;
- How you spend your free time;
- Travelling;
- Discussing your family, friends and colleagues.

Now, let's look at each test individually.

THE IELTS LIFE SKILLS TEST

The IELTS Life Skills Test is 22 minutes long, and has a total of 2 sections. You will take this test along with another test-taker, and share the 22 minutes with them.

During the shared assessment, you will need to discuss and converse with the other person. You will then be marked based on how well you communicate with them. The examiner will judge each of you separately, so you don't need to worry about the other person's performance having a negative impact on your own. That being said, the better and more natural the interaction is between you, the better for the both of you. Therefore, you should make an effort to be friendly to the other person, helping them to relax.

While the examiner will judge you individually, you may still need to do extra things to help your case. For example, if you can't understand what the other test-taker is saying, then always ask them to clarify or repeat. This will mean that your own responses are perfect.

The IELTS Life Skills Test consists of 2 different sections, with smaller parts to each section:

SECTION 1

In the first part of the first section, you will be required to talk with your fellow test-taker, establishing personal facts and asking personal questions. For example, you would ask them about their family and their hobbies.

In the second part of the first section, you will be required to give a short talk on a particular topic, and then each of you will ask the other questions about what they have said. In total, this section lasts for around 10 minutes.

SECTION 2

In the first part of the second section, you will be required to listen to 2 recordings (of people speaking in English) and then answer a number of questions based on these recordings.

In the second part of this section, you'll need to plan an activity (such as a day out to the city) with the other person, and then answer/ask questions about the other person. In total, this section lasts for around 13-15 minutes.

Below we have broken down each of the sections for the IELTS Life Skills Test in more detail:

SECTION 1 – DETAILED BREAKDOWN

The first thing that will happen is that you will enter the exam room, along with the other person taking the test. You'll sit down, and the examiner will introduce themselves to you.

Next, the examiner will start the test. They'll ask both of you some very basic questions, such as 'What is your name? 'Where do you work?' or 'What country do you come from?' You'll then need to ask the other candidate some questions, while the examiner listens. The examiner will give you some topics to choose from, for example family and hobbies; before the other person asks you questions on similar topics. During this time, the examiner may also ask you some questions, which you'll need to answer.

After this, you will be required to give a short 2-minute talk. The examiner will give you the subject that you need to talk about, and provide you with a pen and paper.

You'll have 1 minute before the talk, to write out some notes, which you can then use to help you during your talk. When writing your notes out, try to do them in brief shorthand. Writing whole sentences will slow you down, where you need something that you can just glance at and then carry on speaking. Ideally, you shouldn't just read off the paper either. Make good eye contact with the other 2 people in the room, and speak to them – not into the paper!

Following your talk, the other test-taker will ask you some questions, before giving their own talk. Make sure you listen closely to this talk, as you'll need to ask them questions based on what they've said.

SECTION 2 – DETAILED BREAKDOWN

The second part of the assessment will start with a listening exercise. You will need to listen to a total of 2 recordings, and then answer questions based on these recordings. Whilst you listen to the recordings, you will be able to take notes down on a piece of paper, to help you remember key details. The recordings will usually be generic announcements that you would hear in a building such as a train station.

Following this, you will be asked an initial question or two based on the recordings. This will normally be something along the lines of, 'In which type of building was the first recording made?' The examiner could ask you questions based on either the first or the second recording, so you need to make sure that you listen and make notes on them both.

Next, you will need to listen to the two recordings again, and then answer some more specific questions. To help you with this, before each recording is played, the examiner will tell each of you exactly which pieces of information you need to look out for. Each of you will have a different question to answer, so pay attention to what the examiner is saying.

After this, you will need to plan a scenario with the other test-taker. The examiner will provide you with a leaflet or booklet, and then read out some key information. Following that, you'll need to use this information to make a plan with your partner. For example, you might need to plan a day out to the city of London.

This information read out by the examiner will be useful for your answer. For example, he or she might mention means of transport or particular sights within the city. You will need to use some of these in your discussion, as you consider which options to take. Throughout your discussion, the examiner will be listening closely, to see how strong your levels of English communication are.

For the final part of the test, you will need to ask the other test-taker questions about a certain topic. The examiner will give you the topic beforehand, for example what hobbies the other person has, and you'll then ask each other questions about this.

Summing up...

So, by now you should be able to see, during this test you will need to have a lot of interaction with the other test-taker. Although you might not be a people person, or you might be shy, it is important that the examiner can get a good understanding of your English language capabilities. They need you to speak as much as possible. The more confidently you can speak the language, the better you will do.

Later in this guide, we will run through a number of exercises that are designed to help your language improve.

TRINITY GESE GRADE 5 TEST

The other test that you might choose to take is the Trinity GESE Grade 5 Test. This test can only be taken at an approved centre within the UK.

The Trinity GESE Grade 5 Test is approximately 10 minutes in length.

Unlike the IELTS Life Skills Test, you will not sit this exam with another test-taker, and it will only be you and the examiner in the room. In this test, the examiner will be judging your English-speaking ability against a particular set of criteria.

They'll be making sure that you can do tasks such as:

- Talking about your plans for the future;
- Talking about your preferences, likes and dislikes;
- Talking about certain experiences that you have had;
- Quantifying amounts, for example ordering 2 sandwiches, 3 lemonades.

It shouldn't be too hard to pass this test. Although the idea of being interviewed by someone for 10 minutes might make you nervous, remember that the examiner will want you to succeed, and therefore will try their best to be as helpful to you as possible.

There are two sections in the Trinity GESE Grade 5 Test. In one of them, you will be allowed to discuss a topic of your choice, and in another you will have to engage in a conversation about two separate subjects.

SECTION 1 – DETAILED BREAKDOWN

The first section lasts for 5 minutes. In this task, you will be required to talk about a topic of your choosing. Prior to entering the interview room, you'll be given a piece of paper with a mind-map on it, to help you come up with ideas of things to discuss.

You'll then give this to the examiner, who will look at each circle/box and then ask questions based on what is written in them. You will also need to initiate some discussion with the examiner, so ask them questions based on your topic too; 'Do you like to play video games?' for example.

In terms of what you should talk about, our best advice is to choose something that you are genuinely interested in. After all, the more interested you are, the more you will have to say about that topic.

Remember that the examiner is only interested in how well you can talk (linguistically) about the subject itself, and not in the depth of your knowledge.

<u>There are plenty of things you can choose from here, including:</u>

- **Cooking.** What is your favourite food? What can you cook? What can't you cook?
- **Films.** What is your favourite and least favourite film? Who is your favourite and least favourite actor?
- **TV and other entertainment.** What shows do you watch? Do you play video games?
- **Your family.** How well do you get on with your parents? How many brothers and sisters do you have? Do you live with them?
- **Your job.** What is your job? How long have you worked there? What are your future career plans?
- **Your holiday.** What is your favourite holiday destination? When did you go and for how long? What was your favourite thing about that place?
- **Music.** Who is your favourite band/artist? What is your favourite song? What music do you not like? Have you been to any concerts?
- **Sport.** Do you play sports? Do you support a team? Why do you support them, and do you go to watch them play? Who is your favourite sportsperson?

In each square of your mind map, you can write a few ideas down that relates to the subject you have chosen.

On the next page, we've constructed a sample mind map, to show you how this might look:

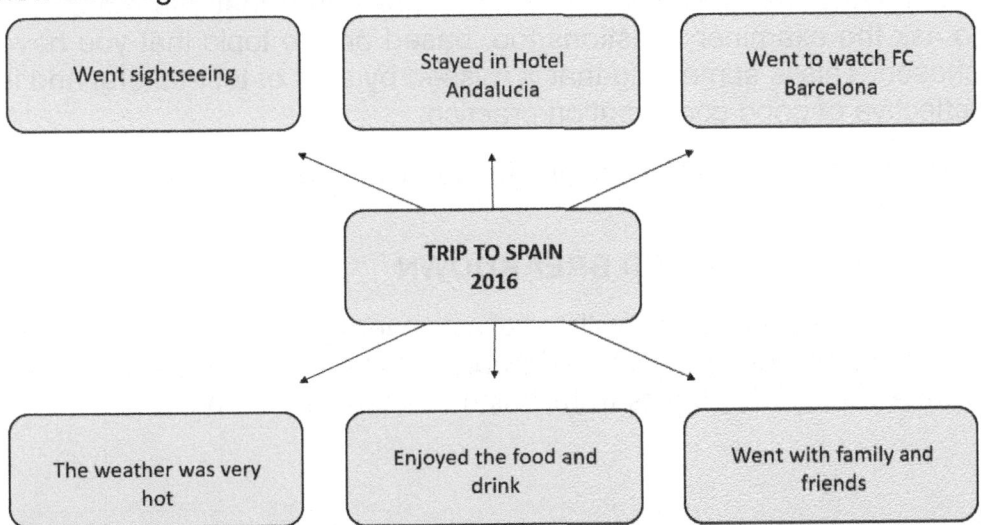

As you can see, these topics allow for continued conversation to be made about different topics.

The examiner will probably pick each circle individually, and ask you questions based on that, so make sure that when you do put something in your mind map, it's something that you know you can talk about.

Looking at our mind map, the questions could include:

- Where in Spain did you stay?
- Did you enjoy the hot weather? Would you prefer somewhere cooler?
- Which friends and family did you go with? Names, your relationship with them, etc.
- Did you make new friends while you were on holiday?
- Where did you go sightseeing? What sights did you see? Can you give your impression of them?
- How was the hotel? Was the service good?
- What type of food did you eat while in Spain?
- How was the football match? Do you support a team? Who is your favourite player? What was the result of the match?

Also, remember that the examiner will be judging you based on how well you interact. This means that you should avoid talking continuously, as this is not how a normal conversation would work. You should pause from time to time, allowing them to ask questions, just as you would with any normal interaction. Likewise, make sure that you remember to ask the examiner questions too, based on the topic that you have chosen. This is something that is missed by a lot of test-takers, and is reflective of good conversation practice.

You'll have approximately 5 minutes to talk, before you move onto the next part of the task.

SECTION 2 – DETAILED BREAKDOWN

In the second task, you will have a conversation with the examiner about two different subjects. This part lasts up to 5 minutes. There are a wide variety of subjects from which the examiner can choose.

Prior to your exam, you will be told what these subjects will be, so that you can prepare for them. In 2016, these included music, transport and personal experiences. You should expect to talk for around 2 to 3 minutes on each subject.

As before, you should make sure that you also ask the examiner questions. For example, 'what is your favourite type of music?'

It's important to ensure that at all times, you are treating the interview as you would a normal conversation. If you don't ask the examiner questions, then you will score poorly, as this is one of the requirements.

The best advice that we can give you for this exam is to prepare at least 2 or 3 questions on each of the subjects, in advance of the test. This means that you won't be caught off guard, and can impress the examiner right from the word go.

Summing up…

Hopefully all of this has given you a better idea of what the differences are between the two tests, and has helped you to decide which one of the tests is the most suitable for you. Now, let's move on to actually preparing for the tests.

CHAPTER 2
Preparing for the B1 Tests

PREPARING FOR THE TESTS

It really is true that practice makes perfect. The more you practice your English before the exam, the easier it will be to speak the language in the exam. Practising your English will also make you more confident, which in turn will lead to better results.

Ideally, the best way to practice is simply to go out and speak to people that you meet. Go to the shops or the cinema, meet with English-speaking friends. You could ask your family or colleagues to only speak to you in English, so that you become more accustomed to the language and don't fall back into speaking in your native language.

IMPROVING YOUR VOCABULARY

One of the biggest things that the examiner will be looking at is your vocabulary. They'll look at the range of words that you can use, and how well you can use them. Although the examiner will be looking for you to demonstrate a good level of proficiency, the marking scheme in this area is fairly relaxed, and B1 examiners will be lenient with a couple of mistakes. However, you should do your absolute best to pronounce and use all the words correctly, as better performance in this area will improve your score.

The variety of your words is also important. The examiner will score you highly for using different words for different topics. For example, saying 'it was nice' about several different things won't score you highly. Saying that one thing 'was great' another 'was awesome' and another 'was fantastic' will score you good marks. You don't have to use really complex words to score highly, but varying up the words that you use will really help you to achieve a good mark. The examiner doesn't want 'yes' or 'no', or simply one word responses – they are looking for a bit more depth. Remember it's all about maintaining a conversation!

So, how can you improve your range of words?

There are plenty of ways to do this. One good way to start off is to create a mind map for each individual subject. Then, once you've done that, add words to the map which relate to the subject. For example, take the word 'shopping', and draw out a mini map with subjects that correlate to this. Under shopping, you could have subjects such as 'what can you buy' – groceries, sweets, bread, pasta, milk. Then draw another column, titled 'how does shopping make you feel?' – bored, excited, hungry, tired, happy. Finally, draw another 1 or 2 columns, to complete your chart. The topics of these could be anything that you associate with shopping, for example 'types of shop' and 'what kind of things you regularly buy'.

Try to write out the list in English if you can. However, if you can't, then simply write them out in your language and then add a translation next to it. Using this technique should help you to expand your vocabulary, and will help you to come up with words that are associated with a particular topic – which is always valuable in everyday English conversation.

Another good way to improve the range of words that you use, is by studying the range of words that *other* people use. You don't have to sound like a walking dictionary, and it's more important to ensure that the words you are using are being used properly, but at the same time you will still need to demonstrate that you have a good vocabulary.

For this reason, books, newspapers and the media will be a great source of inspiration for you. Try and pick newspaper articles that are fairly short in length, and then read over them to try and understand what the writer is saying. Be careful when you are doing this, as some newspapers use shorthand slang to make it easier for their readers. If there are any words that you don't understand, look them up in a dictionary. This can all be done online too, without even needing to purchase a newspaper.

There are numerous news websites out there, all of which you can use to practice. These sites and sources are also a great way of helping you to come to terms with more difficult grammatical concepts, such as tenses and sentence structure.

Remember that while it's important to know the words and demonstrate your vocabulary, you also need to be able to show that you can put these words together. For example, if the examiner asks you a question about going to the cinema, you will need to put together a response which flows properly, instead of just saying words which relate to the cinema. Try and make your responses as natural as possible.

IT'S NOT WHAT YOU SAY, BUT HOW YOU SAY IT

In order to pass the B1 test, you will need to show the examiner not just that you can speak in fluent English, but that you can pronounce and say things in a way that people can understand. Having an accent should not hinder you in this exam, as the examiner will be fully prepared for this and will take it into account when scoring you. This is to be expected, especially if you have lived abroad for most of your life. However, if the examiner cannot understand what you are saying, then this will be a problem. As such, you will need to work hard on improving your pronunciation. There are a number of ways that you can do this.

Firstly, try slowing down the way that you are speaking. Although you should try to keep it natural, slowing down will allow you to speak more clearly and focus on the words that you are saying. Don't be afraid to take a pause in-between sentences. Whether you are pausing to think about what to say, or giving yourself a little breathing room, it's fine. This is completely normal, and reflects everyday speech patterns.

Secondly, listen. It's scientifically proven that the more time you spend in a country, the more likely you are to develop the language habits of that country. With this in mind, the more spoken English you can listen to, the better. Listening to other people pronounce English words should help you learn how to say them. Pay close attention to words and letters which are pronounced in a particular way. Watching TV is a good way to help with this, but at the same time be wary of programmes that use slang words.

Under the B1 requirements, you will be expected to speak and understand what is known as 'Standard English'. Try to watch programmes where the people speak in clear English, ideally without a strong accent. As we mentioned earlier, asking your friends and family to only speak to you in English will go a long way to helping with your own pronunciation.

Thirdly, practise yourself. It goes without saying that you'll need to practise all elements of this test before you go into the exam room; and this is certainly true for your pronunciation. In line with the last point, compare the way that you speak certain words with the way that someone else on television or that you know speaks them. You can record yourself doing this, or ask someone else to provide you with their opinion on how similar it sounds. Then, they'll be able to tell you if you are doing anything wrong.

EXPRESSING YOURSELF

Along with pronunciation and vocabulary, the examiner will also be looking at the way in which you express yourself. Expressing yourself refers to factors such as the way in which you talk, whether you vary your sentence lengths, how many times you pause and how succinctly you put your thoughts and views across.

If in doubt, remember to keep it simple. There is no point in trying to take on complicated and difficult sentences, if you don't have the necessary skills to do this yet. A short, succinct answer, which flows nicely with no breaks, is far better than a jumbled, complex sentence which is full of mistakes and pauses between words. The examiner won't expect you to take on really difficult subjects, so don't worry about this.

This is one of the reasons that practising your speech beforehand will be so helpful. Through practice, you will pick up certain words or phrases which you'll find yourself using or repeating. You can use these phrases in the exam, if not as a first response, but as a fall back response. It's always good to have words or phrases that you are comfortable with. The more comfortable you are, the better and more confident you will sound, and this will impress the examiner.

Expression also refers to the fluidity of your sentences. While it's okay to have short stops and pauses occasionally, too many of these will detract from what you are saying and will hurt your test score. This is especially the case during times when you are required to give a short talk. Since you will be (mostly) speaking continuously for this exercise, it's important that you can manage the way you speak.

If you have ever had to deliver a presentation, whether for work or educational purposes, then you will have a good idea of what we mean here. You need to consider your audience. If you haven't had to deliver a presentation before, then you may have been in the audience listening to one. Think about what techniques the speaker used to communicate with their audience. Methods such as eye contact, hand gestures, and speaking clearly and slowly are always good. You can also acknowledge the audience, in this case the other test-taker and the examiner by asking questions such as 'are you following?' or 'have you understood everything so far?' There is nothing wrong with this, and the examiner will appreciate you taking the time to ask, as well as being impressed by your English skills.

Another method that is also useful for presentations applies here: if you make a mistake, don't stop or panic. Just brush over it and keep going! Take a second to compose yourself, and keep talking.

If the examiner wishes to question you on the mistake, then they'll do so at the end, rather than letting it derail the rest of your talk. Of course, if you are able to, you can always quickly add, 'Oh, my mistake, I meant…' before swiftly moving on, but don't allow that mistake to bring the talk to a complete standstill while you are trying to correct it.

Remember that small pauses are okay. At B1 level, it is expected that there will be short pauses, and that you'll make one or two minor mistakes, so take your time and focus on speaking as clearly and correctly as possible.

LISTENING AND INTERACTING

As we have mentioned, interacting with the examiner and the other test-taker is very important. With this in mind, it's very important that you don't lose focus, and concentrate 100% on the task at hand. You can't afford to start daydreaming or lose track, as the examiner and the other test-taker will be asking you to respond to them. At all times, make sure that you are polite and formal. The exam room is no place to use slang terms.

Along with making sure that you listen closely to what is being said, you will also need to be an active participant. Obviously, you should never interrupt the other person, but it's a good idea to demonstrate basic conversational reaction skills. For example, making comments to show your emotion, such as 'that's great!' or 'really?' Obviously, you should only do this if you are confident in knowing what the other person said, otherwise you could make a mistake and be penalised.

When it comes to listening, the examiner will also take into account the speed at which the other person talks. So, if the other person is talking too fast for you to understand, then they won't penalise you for this. However, you could be penalised if you fail to bring it to their attention, so make sure you do. Just a small interruption such as 'sorry, I didn't quite catch that, please could you repeat it more slowly?' works just fine. During the recordings that you will have to listen to during the Life Skills Test, the people in the recordings will be speaking slowly and clearly in Standard English, so you won't have to worry about this.

A good way to practice your listening is simply to just go out in public, and listen to what is being said around you. Obviously, we aren't recommending that you start eavesdropping on other people's conversations, but you should be able to pick up smaller elements of basic conversation, such as communicating with a shopkeeper, asking a supermarket assistant for help, etc. All of this will ultimately contribute to your ability to listen during the exam, and then respond to what is being said in the right way. In the real world, people don't always speak slowly and clearly, or in Standard English. Often they will mumble, speak quickly or speak in slang. Remember that while English is arguably a fairly easy language to learn, it is also different from many other languages, in that it contains a lot of silent letters. This can make pronunciation quite difficult for newcomers. Over time, you will become accustomed to this.

When studying for the exam, it is advised that you dedicate a significant portion of your spare time to watching English speaking movies, television shows or reading books. Ideally, in the former two, you should try not to have the subtitles on, or at the very least work towards this aim. If you wish for further practice, there are a number of online resources at your disposal.

Arguably the best of these is the British Council website, which contains numerous recordings designed to help B1 learners. For more information on this, please check out the following website: https://www.britishcouncil.org/english.

Now that we've looked at some language preparation tips, let's move onto planning for the language practicalities of the exam.

CHAPTER 3
Exam Language

UNDERSTANDING THE LANGUAGE

During the test, the examiner will be trying to establish whether you are able to speak English to the required B1 standard. As mentioned, the language criteria that you will need to meet in order to pass this test, is not all that difficult. You will simply need to show that you can function as part of British society.

In this section of the book, we'll break down particular areas of the exam, and give you some sample questions that you might face. The questions listed in this chapter could be asked during any of the assessments, and could be either from your fellow test-taker, or from the examiner. Along with this, you might find that this section provides you with useful questions that you yourself might ask your fellow test-taker.

Please note, the questions listed in this section are for practice purposes only, and are not the exact same questions that you will be asked during the exam.

TYPICAL B1 QUESTIONS AND TOPICS

Personal Questions

This is usually the standard introductory topic, but don't worry, the examiner won't get too personal.

In this section, you'll be asked questions including:

- What is your name?
- Which country do you come from?
- How old are you?
- Do you have any children?
- Do you have any brothers and sisters?
- Tell me about your mother.
- Tell me about your father.

Some of these questions will focus specifically around the past, and require you to demonstrate use/knowledge of the past tense.

For example, you might be asked:

- What did you do last weekend?
- What was your favourite game as a child?
- Where did you grow up?
- When did you move to the UK?

In these cases, you'll have to use the past tense – was/went/etc. – to respond. For example, 'I was born in France' or 'last weekend I went to the cinema'.

Your likes and dislikes

In this section, you'll be asked questions based around your likes and dislikes.

This could include questions such as:

- What is your favourite film?
- What is your favourite food?
- What is your least favourite form of travel?
- Do you play any sports? Which do you like best?

The key to answering questions from this section is to expand and elaborate on your responses. For example, if the examiner asks 'what is your favourite film?' then don't just say 'Titanic' or 'my favourite film is Titanic.' A better response would be 'Titanic is my favourite film, because I enjoy the romance and the historical aspect.'

If you give a monotone or simplistic response, then the examiner will prompt you to explain why it's your favourite/least favourite, so by doing this yourself you can avoid them having to prompt you – and gain extra marks in the process!

At many points, you can expect questions from different sections to mix. For example, you might be asked 'what is your favourite thing about your job?' This question is two-fold, and requires you to take the initiative in explaining where you work, and then following this up by explaining what your favourite thing about the job is.

This section also intercedes with hobbies, as you could easily be asked questions such as:

- What is your favourite thing to do in your free time?
- What is your favourite type of music to listen to?
- Do you share any hobbies with other family members?
- Are there any hobbies which you had as a child, which you still pursue now?
- Why do you think having a hobby is important? If you don't, why not?
- Tell me about favourite hobby. How often do you do it and what does it entail?
- How do you feel about going to the cinema?
- Before you moved to England, what did you do in your spare time?
- Do you spend much time browsing the internet? If so, what are your favourite sites?
- Do you follow the news?
- Do you have a favourite channel on TV that you like to watch?

In all cases, make sure you provide an answer that doesn't just answer the question, but gives the examiner some extra info too.

Shopping

Shopping, and buying items, is a very popular topic in the assessment. This is because this subject focuses around something that is a necessary requirement in everyday British life – going to the shops and buying things like food or other essentials.

With this in mind, the examiner will want confirmation that you are fully capable of doing this.

The questions could include:

CHAPTER 3   Exam Language   37

- How often do you visit the local supermarket?
- How does going to the supermarket make you feel?
- Do you often go out clothes shopping?
- What is your favourite brand of clothing?
- Is there anything unusual that you often buy from the supermarket?
- Do you have any expensive purchases that you have lined up for the future?
- Are you saving for anything?
- What supermarket do you normally shop at? Why? Are there any supermarkets that you don't like?

Future plans

In this section, you'll be asked questions based around the future, and some questions based around future predictions. You'll need to use the future tense – will/shall/going to – to answer.

The questions could include:

- What are your plans for this weekend?
- When will you next see your family?
- When do you think humans will become extinct?

Don't worry, this section doesn't require you to brush up on any extra-curricular knowledge, all of the questions regarding the future will be fairly simple and on topics which you don't necessarily need to have lived in England to have thought about.

However, it's always helpful to have some extra knowledge, as there is a chance that you could be asked questions such as:

- Who do you think will win the next Wimbledon Championships?
- Who do you think will win the next football World Cup?

If you aren't a follower of football or tennis, then you can simply say to the examiner, 'I'm sorry, I don't follow this sport', or to the football question you can simply say, 'I think Spain will win the World Cup'. If the examiner asks you to justify this, simply respond with 'they have the best players and the best team.' So, as you can see, the examiner won't expect you to go too in-depth during these types of questions.

The examiner may also ask you questions based around chance and possibility, for example:

- Is there a good chance of that happening?
- How likely is that?
- How sure are you?
- Can you make that a possibility?

In this scenario, you should try to answer in as much detail as possible, whilst justifying this too. For example, 'yes, I think Spain are very likely to win the World Cup, as they have great players and a great manager' or, 'while it is very unlikely that I will ever become a professional football player, I will do my best to accomplish this.'

Reasoning and justification

At many points in the exam, the examiner will ask you to justify or explain the things that you have said.

This will usually be in response to an answer that you have just given, for example:

- Why do you think that is?
- Why do you believe that happened?
- Was there a reason for this?
- What was the cause of this?

As mentioned, you can avoid these questions altogether by explaining your answer in full. This is reflective of everyday conversation style, where people pre-emptively explain themselves to save the other person asking them why. If the examiner does want you to explain further still, or hasn't quite understood, they'll ask something along the lines of:

- Can you explain that?
- What do you mean?
- Could you provide me with an explanation?

Your experiences

You'll be asked a lot of questions based around your experiences, and this is a common part of British life, so be ready to answer questions on them.

When telling the examiner about your experiences, try and be as detailed as possible. For example, if the examiner asks, 'do you like going to the seaside?' then don't say just 'yes'. A better answer would be, 'yes, I find that the seaside is very calm and comforting, I really like the sea and would love to live by the coast someday' or 'no, I don't like the smell of the sea or how windy the coast gets. I much prefer the city.'

Other questions could include:

- Tell me about a recent trip that you went on.
- What did you do for your last birthday?
- Have you been to any birthday parties or celebrations lately?
- Where was the last place that you visited with your friends?
- Do you ever go out to nightclubs?
- What is your favourite restaurant?
- Are you very active at the weekends, or do you prefer to stay in?

When answering these questions, the more detail you can provide the better. Just as with the other sections, an answer such as 'for my last birthday I went to France' won't really suffice. You need to give a detailed response to this question, such as, 'for my last birthday I went to France, with my family. We went out to a restaurant and then stayed in the Hotel Le Chaliesse.' Be prepared to give your opinion on these experiences too. The examiner might ask questions such as, 'did you enjoy that?' or 'how did it go?'

Your home

This is quite a common area, so be ready to answer a variety of questions based on where you live at the time of testing. As ever, the more detail you can give, the better.

This is especially the case for questions such as: 'describe your house to me'. In this case, a good answer would be something like, 'I live in a two floor, semi-detached house. We have a front garden and a back garden. My house is in an avenue; so there are many other houses on the same street. Inside the house, we have 4 bedrooms, two bathrooms and a kitchen joined to the lounge. The house is new and modern.'

The examiner might also ask questions such as:

- Apart from you, who else lives in your house?
- Do you rent or own your house?
- Do you get on with your neighbours?
- Do you like spending time at home?
- If you do still live with your parents, do you have plans to buy your own home?
- Do you have any plans to make changes to your home?
- How does your home now, compare to the home where you grew up?

Travelling

Travelling and transportation are frequently used topics during the assessment, so be ready to answer questions based on this topic.

The questions could even relate to your journey to the assessment centre, for example:

- How did you get here today? How was your journey?

- Did you plan your route before the day?

You'll also be asked questions based on your regular daily schedule, for example:

- What is the most common form of transport that you take?
- Do you have a bus pass?
- How long is your journey into work each day?

Along with general questions about travelling in Britain, the examiner will also ask you questions about travelling elsewhere, taking holidays etc. For these questions, you will do well to elaborate a little more. For example, if the examiner asks, 'have you visited any other countries recently?' you should answer with something akin to, 'yes, last year I went to Japan with my mother and father. We stayed in a hotel in Tokyo'. As we explained before, the more detail you can give, the better.

Other questions might include:

- Which airline company is your favourite to travel with?
- Have you visited many other places in Britain?
- How many holidays do you take a year?
- Do you like going abroad during the summer, or would you prefer to stay at home?

As before, you can expect topics such as this to interlink with subjects such as past, present, future and preferences, for example:

- What would be your dream place to visit?
- What is your favourite place that you have visited? Do you have any plans to go back? What did you like about this place?
- Have you ever visited somewhere abroad and not enjoyed it? If so, where?

- Do you prefer to go on holiday with family or friends?

Family and friends

This is a very common topic in the exam, so be prepared to discuss this with both your fellow test-taker and the examiner.

The questions will include:

- Are you married or in a relationship?
- Do you spend lots of time with your family?
- Who is your closest friend? Do you have a lot of friends?
- What kind of activities do you do with your friends?

Sometimes, the examiner won't ask you questions that are directly about yourself. You need to be ready to answer different kinds of questions fluently. For example, the examiner might ask 'why is it important to have close friends?' The purpose of this question is two-fold. Firstly, they want to check that you are able to discuss general issues, not just including talking about yourself. Secondly, these kinds of questions are designed to test you a little further than what many people may have prepared for.

So remember, the test isn't just about you and yourself, you'll need to answer some general questions too. A good response to this type of question would be: 'It's important for people to have friends, as friends make you happy. Spending time with friends is the best way to use the time when you are not working. The more time you spend with friends, the more relaxed and happier you will feel.'

Your work and education

Another very common topic in the exam, is your work and education. As mentioned, the examiner will be talking to you about general topics of everyday conversation.

People in Britain spend a lot of time talking about their work, so it is important that you are able to articulate yourself clearly in this subject area.

There are a wide variety of questions that you could be asked in this

area, including:
- Where did you go to school?
- Did you enjoy school? If so, why? If not, why not?
- Did you go to university? If so, where did you go, and did you enjoy it?
- Do you think that education is important?
- What kind of school do your children go to?

The examiner may also ask you questions about your choice of work or speciality, for example:
- What made you decide to work at this company?
- Why did you decide to go into this line of work?
- Tell me about what kind of things you have to do for your job.
- Does the company that you work for have a website?
- Do you see this as a long-term position?
- Have you completed any extra training alongside your current job?
- How long have you been working in this job?
- What kind of job did you have before you moved to England?
- Does your job interest you, or is it simply a way to pay the bills?

Professional relationships are also a focus in this section, and you'll be asked questions such as:
- Do you get on with your work colleagues?
- Are you still friends with anyone from school?
- Do you ever see your work colleagues outside of work?

Health and fitness

Health and fitness is another popular topic in the exam, and there are plenty of questions that you could be asked in this section. Remember, however, that the examiner is only judging you based on the quality of your responses. So, if the examiner asks, 'do you consider yourself to be a fit and healthy person?' it's okay to say no, as long as you justify your response. For example, 'no, I don't exercise; and I am a heavy smoker' is just as acceptable as 'yes, I go jogging three times a day.' Of course, however, the examiner will also ask you questions based around the positive aspects of exercise too, even if you say no.

They might ask:

- What are the benefits of exercise?
- Do you not like to exercise? If not, why not?
- Did you exercise in the past? If so, what kind of things did you do?

The examiner might also ask you general questions regarding health and fitness, for example:

- Is there a gym in your area?
- What is your opinion of the National Health Service (NHS)?
- Have you ever had to visit a doctor or hospital in the UK? What was your experience like?
- Do you try to eat healthily? What kinds of food do you eat?

Now that we've looked at the questions you might be asked, and the potential topics which could come up, let's move on to the language that you'll need to demonstrate.

YOUR RESPONSES

Naturally, the most important element in you passing the B1 test, is in the overall quality of your responses. Throughout the exam, you'll be asked direct questions by the examiner, and possibly another test-taker too (if you are sitting the exam with them). There are a number of ways

CHAPTER 3 Exam Language

to guarantee that you give a good quality response to the questions.

Firstly, let's look at what a good quality response actually is, and isn't.

A **good** response is an answer which:

- Demonstrates your ability to speak at B1 level;
- Shows that you have understood the question;
- Contains only a few or no grammatical errors;
- Uses a good range of words and vocabulary.

Here's an example of a good response:

Q. 'Do you like to go to the cinema?'

A. 'Yes, I love going to the cinema. Just last week I went with my friends to see the new superhero movie. We didn't enjoy the film so much, but we still had a great time.'

On the other hand, **a bad response** is an answer which:

- Is very short and monotone, does not give the examiner a chance to see your language skills.
- Does not really answer the question that has been asked.
- Contains problems with tenses, verbs, pronouns etc.
- Uses repetitive language.

Here's an example of a bad response:

Q. 'Do you like going to the cinema?'

A. 'Yes, I like going to the cinema.'

As we have mentioned several times, the more you say in your answer, the better. The reason for this is that the more you say, the more language skills you are showing to the examiner, and the more evidence they will have that you can speak at B1 level.

Later in this book, we'll give you some practice on how to answer some test related questions.

Along with this, the examiner will also require you to demonstrate that you can use particular English language techniques.

EXPRESS TO IMPRESS

The examiner will want to know that you can demonstrate certain elements of the English language. That is to say, you will need to show an ability to do things such as asking questions, persuading, suggesting and giving your opinion.

In the English language, there are certain words and phrases that we use to indicate what we are saying/trying to do. For example, if I was making a suggestion, I might start by saying, 'have you considered...?' This is a natural language technique, and makes your suggestion easier to understand/accept. If I simply said, 'you must do this!' instead of 'have you considered doing this?' then the meaning of what I'm saying is drastically altered. Instead of making a polite suggestion, I am giving a command, which could come across as rude.

Below we have broken down many of these language techniques into smaller sub-sections, to help you understand them better.

GIVING OPINIONS

Giving your opinion is a really important part of the examination. The examiner will want to see that you are able to put across your own views, in a polite and acceptable manner. There are many ways that you can begin a sentence where you are offering your opinion.

These include:

- In my opinion…
- I feel that…
- The way I see it…
- Personally, I am of the opinion that…
- I think that…

- It seems to me like…
- From my perspective…

AGREEING AND DISAGREEING

This is another important part of the exam, especially if you are in the room with another test-taker. You need to be able to agree with them on certain points, and politely disagree where necessary. The key word here being 'politely'. Obviously, you don't want to get into a big argument with the other test-taker, but at the same time don't agree with them for the sake of it.

The examiner will score you highly for putting yourself across politely, even if you don't agree with the other person. There are many ways that you can begin a sentence showing that you agree or disagree.

These include:

- I agree!
- I couldn't agree more.
- You are so right.
- I feel the same way.
- I'm not sure about that.
- I don't think that's correct.
- I really disagree with you.
- I'm afraid I don't agree.
- I'm almost the exact opposite.

SEEKING CLARIFICATION

At many times during the exam, you might need to seek clarification on something that has been said. This is absolutely okay, and the examiner will score you higher for making use of your language skills in seeking clarification, than they will for you ignoring it and pretending to understand. The chances are, the latter option will involve you giving an incorrect answer, so this won't help you. There are many ways to question or seek clarification on something.

They include:

- Please could repeat that? I didn't quite catch what you said.
- Sorry, I don't understand.
- Could you explain that a little further?
- I don't follow what you are saying.
- Sorry, please could you repeat that?
- So, do you mean….?

ASKING QUESTIONS

Naturally, when you are in the exam, you'll need to be asking the other person questions. Just as with offering opinions, it's polite to frame your questions with a statement before. This makes them less direct, and a little less scary to answer.

There are plenty of ways to do this:

- I'm wondering…
- Please could you tell me…?
- Please could you share with me…?
- What about…?
- Tell me about…

PERSUASION

Persuading, politely, is a natural part of everyday conversation. This is very similar to offering your opinion, except here you are trying to persuade the person to do a certain thing.

A good example could be this: Imagine that you are in the testing room, with another test-taker. The other test-taker is very shy. You lead the conversation, but they are reluctant to follow up on your ideas. What words and phrases would you use to try and persuade them to open up and talk to you?

You could use phrases such as:

- Come on, let's do it, it will be really interesting.
- I think this will definitely work out well.
- I think this is a really good idea, don't you?
- I think this is the best course of action.
- You'll definitely enjoy it.
- It will be really fun, let's give it a go.

COMPARISONS

Making comparisons is a common element of everyday conversation, and you will often find British people comparing and contrasting things when they speak. For example, they might say, 'the weather today is much worse than yesterday'.

There are plenty of ways that you can do this, and comparisons will help you to achieve high marks in your test:

- Comparatively speaking, I'd say…
- This one seems much bigger than that one.
- It's more interesting than…
- I preferred it to…
- In contrast, my one is…
- On the other hand…

POSSIBILITY AND SPECULATION

Speculating about future events is a normal part of everyday British language. During the exam, there is a possibility that you might be asked a question such as 'and how likely do you think that is to happen?' or 'what are the chances of that?' You'll need to be able to answer in a way that demonstrates your ability to talk about chance and possibility.

For example:

- There is a good chance that this will happen.
- No, I think the chances are very low.
- It's quite possible.
- It's almost impossible.
- I'm fairly certain about it.
- I'm feeling positive about it.
- I don't think the chances are very high.

TOP TIPS TO ACE YOUR TEST

Now that you've arrived at the day of the exam, you might well be feeling quite nervous. Don't worry, this is completely normal. The people at the test centre will make you feel extremely welcome.

Along with this, provided you have prepared well, you should have no problem passing the assessment. With that being said however, it never hurts to have a few extra tips.

So, here are our top tips for passing the assessment:

Plan your route

- This is really important. If you are late for the test, you will need to pay for another test on a separate date. With this in mind, plan your route in advance of the day.

- Work out elements such as parking, transport and how long it will take to get to the test centre. You then won't have to worry about these things on the day in question.

- Along with this, make sure that you have all of your essential documents, like your passport, ready in a folder. The more of this you get sorted, the easier it will be to just focus on the test and achieve good marks.

CHAPTER 3   Exam Language

- You will be allowed into the test centre 30 minutes before the test actually starts, so plan for this too.

Focus on your words

- One mistake that some candidates make, is that they allow themselves to become distracted by the occasion. Some candidates will go into the room, and instead of giving clear and concise answers; will allow themselves to worry too much about their notes, the examiner or the other test-taker. Focus on yourself!

- Your focus needs to be on your own performance, and making sure that you are speaking as clearly and carefully as possible.

Don't be afraid to ask for clarification

- Another common mistake is being scared to ask the examiner or the other test-taker to repeat information.

- Many people fear that they'll be marked down for this, when in fact the opposite is true.

- By asking for clarification, you are actually meeting a part of the marking criteria. You'll gain much higher marks for questioning and then producing a high-quality response, than you would for failing to understand and then offering a low-quality response.

Practise your speaking

- If you are feeling really nervous, it's all too easy to lose track of what you are saying.

- A common problem that people who are nervous face, is that they start talking too fast, and then it becomes difficult to understand them.

- This is why you need to practise your speaking first. Obviously, you won't be able to capture the exact exam conditions, or reflect the pressure of the day, but the more time you spend speaking in English, the more comfortable you will be during the exam.

Ask questions

- Although you will mostly be preparing to talk about yourself in the exam, remember that you also need to be able to ask the other person questions, or the examiner.

- Conversation is two-way, so you need to make an effort to plan and ask your own questions too.

- Try and approach this as you would any normal conversation. Be polite and considerate of the other person, try not to interrupt when they are speaking, and greet them in a friendly manner when you first meet.

Practise your talk

- The short talk part of the assessment is perhaps the easiest to prepare for, so you shouldn't have too many problems with this.

- Make sure that your talk has enough material to last for at least 5 minutes.

- A good way to practise your talk is to give it to your friends and family, and then have them ask you questions in English.

Memorise terms

- This is one of the most important, and obvious, things that you need to do when preparing for the exam.

- Obviously, if you don't know key terms, then you will struggle to speak in the exam. This requires basic revision – and there are plenty of ways to do this. Anything from post-it notes to online revision guides, even this study book!

- There are an enormous number of revision resources out there for you, so make full use of them!

Now, have a go at the practice tests, to see how well you've learned.

CHAPTER 4
Practice Tests

PRACTICE TEST QUESTIONS AND ANSWERS

Each of the below tests will test you on something different, or require you to use different means to come up with the answer. Have a go at all of these tests, before comparing your answers with the ones at the back of the book.

Below we've provided you with an example of how to answer each type of question that you'll encounter in these tests. You should refer back to these examples if you get stuck on how to do them.

*Please note, these are not the actual questions that you will face in the exam, they are simply to help you practise your language skills.

RESPONDING TO QUESTIONS

The first type of question that you'll see in our mock tests, requires you to pick the best response from a selection of answers.

For example, you might see a question such as this:

What was your favourite activity to do when you were a child?

You'll then be given a selection of answers, like so:

A – When I was a child, I liked to play tennis with my father.

B – I played tennis.

C – Nowadays, I like to play squash with my friends.

D – Tennis.

All you need to do, is pick the best answer from the list. This one is fairly easy. Option C doesn't answer the question, and options B and D are too short – so won't constitute a good response. Therefore, the answer is A.

CHAPTER 4 *Practice Tests* 55

COMPLETING THE MISSING LINE

The next type of question that you'll see in our mock tests, requires you to complete the missing line from a conversation. Again, you'll need to pick the best option from a selection of answers.

For example, you might see something like this:

> Speaker A: Last week, I went to the doctors. It was quite a scary experience.
>
> Speaker B: Oh no, how come? Are you ill?
>
> Speaker A:
>
> Speaker B: Oh, what a relief, I'm really glad about that.

As you can see, there is a gap where Speaker A should have responded. You will need to pick which answer option best fits in the gap. Pay close attention to how Speaker B has responded, because this should influence which answer option you pick:

A – Extremely. Unfortunately, the doctor has told me that I don't have long to live.

B – I was having severe headaches. Luckily the doctor diagnosed me as healthy.

C – After that, I played football with my friends.

D – I'm still having headaches.

The best answer option here is B. You can see that Speaker B has responded with 'what a relief, I'm really glad'. This is not something they would say if we'd picked answer option A or option D. Meanwhile, C doesn't answer the question.

INCORRECT WORDS

This type of question is fairly simple to complete.

You'll be given a conversation between two speakers, for example:

> Speaker A: After this assessment, I'm going to meet my friend.
>
> Speaker B: Oh great, what are you going to do?
>
> Speaker A: We're probably going to go to the cinema, to see the new romance movie.
>
> Speaker B: That sounds like a lot of fun. I went to the headphones last week.

If you look at this conversation, the last line doesn't make sense. The word 'headphones' shouldn't be there. Now look at the below answer options, and decide which word would be the best to replace it:

A – Betting

B – Cinema

C – Brown

D – Lorry

The best word in this instance would be 'Cinema'. So, the answer is B.

Another variation on this type of question, which you'll see during our mock tests, requires you to identify the word that is incorrect.

For example:

> Matthew went to the park and bought a tinfoil from the food booth.

A – Matthew

B – Tinfoil

C – Booth

D – Food

In this case, the answer would be 'tinfoil', as this is clearly incorrectly placed in the sentence.

CHAPTER 4 — Practice Tests

COMPLETE THE NEXT LINE

For this type of question, you'll be given a sentence.

For example:

> *Next week, I am going to visit London with my friend. We will go out for dinner and then visit a bar.*

Your job is to complete the next sentence, using the answer options provided:

A – I was really excited for it.

B – I couldn't wait!

C – I'm really looking forward to it.

The answer here is C, as this is written in the future tense, which matches with the question.

REPLACE THE WORD

This type of question is very easy to complete. All you need to do, is replace the word written in capital letters, with the correct word from the answer options.

For example:

> *Last week, I went to visit my mother in hospital. Unfortunately, she is very BALLOON.*

A – Raisin

B – Lions

C – Sick

D – Orange

The best answer here is C, as none of the other words would make sense in this sentence.

CHAPTER 4

Practice Tests

REPLACE THE SENTENCE

In this type of question, you will be given a poorly worded sentence. You'll need to decide which answer option best replaces the sentence.

<u>For example:</u>

> *On Wednesday, I am going to buy a potty for my child. I was really excited to buy it, as it is an exciting time in my child's life.*

A – On Wednesday, I am going to buy a potty for my child. I am really excited to buy it, as it is an exciting time in my child's life.

B – On Wednesday, I am going to buy a potty for my child. I will be really excited to buy it, as it was an exciting time in my child's life.

The best answer option here is A, as it uses tenses correctly, unlike option B.

Now, have a go at the mock tests.

TEST 1

QUESTION 1

What are your future career plans? Do you have any ambitions to move on from your current job?

A – I love my job, but I won't do it for the rest of my life.

B – I am a very ambitious person. I want to become a lawyer one day.

C – I love my job, but one day I hope to become a successful lawyer. I cannot stay at this company forever.

D – My job is great, but I am ambitious. I want to become a lawyer.

QUESTION 2

I believe that integrity is more important than winning. If you win without integrity, you may as well be SURFING.

A – Broken.

B – Losing.

C – Frowning.

D – Dead.

QUESTION 3

> Speaker A: Are there any hobbies that you'd really like to try in the future?
>
> Speaker B: I'd love to learn how to ice skate.
>
> Speaker A: Ice skating, how interesting! Why do you want to learn that?
>
> Speaker B:

A – Football players earn lots of money. I'd like to do the same.

B – Ice skating is a very graceful sport. It's a bit like dancing.

C – It looks fun.

D – Why do you want to learn how to play tennis?

QUESTION 4

> What kind of music do you listen to?

A – I don't like music, it's boring. I'd rather play with the tools in my shed.

B – Yep, music is a great concept.

C – I listen to lots of 90s music. Especially songs that have appeared in films.

D – Somebody once told me that music is a waste of time.

QUESTION 5

How do you get to work in the mornings?

A – Train.

B – I take the train from Charing Cross Station to London Victoria, and from there I catch a bus to my office.

C – I get the train and then the bus.

D – I get a bus from the train station.

QUESTION 6

When you aren't working, what kind of things do you do in your free time?

A – I am always working.

B – I play video games.

C – I enjoy playing poker online. Last Sunday I made lots of money.

D – In my free time I like to sit in front of the TV.

CHAPTER 4　　　　　　　　Practice Tests　　　63

QUESTION 7

> Speaker A: It's really nice to meet you. What have you been up to this past weekend?
>
> Speaker B: Doing bits buddy, and you?
>
> Speaker A: Well I went to see my grandmother on Sunday, unfortunately she's terribly ill.
>
> Speaker B: I'm delighted to hear that.

A – Weekend.

B – Unfortunately.

C – Terribly.

D – Sorry.

QUESTION 8

> What do you think about the National Health Service (NHS)?

A – The NHS is a great service. In my country, you have to pay for medical care.

B – The NHS is very slow.

C – I admire the staff who work at the NHS.

D – One day, I would love to become a doctor, and this is what I'm currently training for.

QUESTION 9

> My grandmother dies last week. In two days' time, I will attend her funeral.

A – I attended the funeral of my grandmother last week.

B – I am attend the funeral of my grandmother next week.

C – I would attend the funeral of my grandmother next week.

QUESTION 10

> Gemma packs the boxes but she did it slow and is fired.

A – Gemma packed the boxes, but she did it slowly, and was fired.

B – Gemma packed the boxes, but she did it slow, and is fired.

QUESTION 11

> Since you moved to England, have you tried any takeaway restaurants?

A – Yes.

B – Pizza.

C – I tried pizza. I didn't like it.

D – Yes, I tried pizza. Unfortunately, the place that we ordered from wasn't so good.

QUESTION 12

> I went to the doctors, complaining about a FUNKY. He provided me with antibiotics.

A – Sand.

B – Beef.

C – Cough.

D – Henry.

CHAPTER 4 Practice Tests 65

QUESTION 13

I believe that the internet is a dangerous place for children. They should not be MUSTARD to go on there.

A – When.

B – Allowed.

C – Seen.

D – Because.

QUESTION 14

Speaker A: Unfortunately, I'm not very good with money. My account manager keeps telling me to stop spending it on clothes.

Speaker B: Ha ha, oh dear. I'm very good with money, luckily.

Speaker A: What do you normally spend your money on?

Speaker B:

Speaker A: Ah, that's very kind of you.

A – Usually I spend my money on essentials like food and drink, and then save the rest.

B – I spent a bit on food and drink, and then gamble the rest in the casino.

C – I give a lot of my money to charity.

D – I just don't spend it.

QUESTION 15

Are you married? Tell me about your partner.

A – I have been married for 4 years now. My partner is named Michael, and he works in a printing shop.

B – Yes, I have been married for 4 years as of next week.

C – My partner is named Michael. He is rich.

D – Yes, we have been married for 4 years. Soon we will divorce.

CHAPTER 4 Practice Tests

TEST 2

QUESTION 1

Speaker A: That's great to hear that you completed your degree. What are your future career plans?

Speaker B: Well, I'd like to write my own book.

Speaker A: How exciting, do you have any ideas for what you'll write about?

Speaker B: Not at the moment. How about you, what are your career plans?

Speaker A:

A – Well, after I leave here today I'm planning on going shopping with my mother.

B – Tonight I'll sit down and watch the news.

C – I already have a job.

D – I would love to be a professional interior designer. I like drawing and making things.

QUESTION 2

Yesterday, I went into the shops and bought a jacket and jeans. Unfortunately, the jacket was too PLASTIC for my liking, and the jeans were very ugly. I should have tried them on before I purchased them.

A – Big.

B – Watery.

C – Fruity.

D – Cold.

QUESTION 3

Somebody once ask me to borrow money, as they have run out of change for gas.

A – Somebody once ask me to borrow money, as they had run out of gas.

B – Somebody once asked me to borrow money, as they had run out of change for gas.

QUESTION 4

What do you think of the UK train system?

A – It is bad.

B – Trains are always late in the UK.

C – I don't take the train.

D – UK train journeys are extremely expensive compared to elsewhere, and the service is bad.

QUESTION 5

Speaker A: It's great that you spend so much time with your friends.
Speaker B: I know, I'm very lucky to have such good friends. How about you, do you see your friends a lot?
Speaker A:
Speaker B: That's a shame.

A – No, most of them live back in my own country.

B – Yes, all the time. I live with 2 of them.

C – Friends are an expendable commodity.

D – Yes.

CHAPTER 4   Practice Tests   69

QUESTION 6

> When I was a child, my father took me to the zoo. Unfortunately he was WEDDING by tigers.

A – Drank.

B – Eaten.

C – Paid.

D – Raised.

QUESTION 7

> What is the one thing that you miss more than anything, since moving to England?

A – England is much better than my own country.

B – Although I love England, I miss my family, who stayed back at home.

C – The hot weather.

D – The food here is bland and uninteresting.

QUESTION 8

> Ice skating was a dangerous sport. You could fell down and hurt yourself.

A – Ice skating is a dangerous sport. You could fallen down and hurt yourself.

B – Ice skating is a dangerous sport. You could fall down and hurt yourself.

QUESTION 9

Speaker A: I've been in hospital for the past 2 weeks, with a serious medical condition.

Speaker B: Oh no, are you okay now though?

Speaker A: Yes, thank you. The NHS were extremely terrible, they took such good care of me.

Speaker B: I'm glad to hear it.

A – Medical.

B – Care.

C – Terrible.

D – Condition.

QUESTION 10

How do you find the weather in England?

A – Rainy!

B – It's very cold here compared to my own country.

C – Quite warm.

D – I find that people in England talk about the weather a lot.

CHAPTER 4 Practice Tests 71

QUESTION 11

Speaker A: I love going to the cinema. My favourite types of movies are comedies.

Speaker B: Oh, I love the cinema too. I like comedies, but my favourite type of film is action.

Speaker A: Did you see the new action film that is out? I heard that it's terrible.

Speaker B: Yes, I went to see it last week. You are right, me and my friends thought it was fantastic.

Speaker A: Yes, my friend went to see it and told me that he really didn't enjoy it.

A – Fantastic.

B – Comedies.

C – Enjoy.

D – Cinema.

QUESTION 12

I do not feel comfortable dancing in nightclubs. There are too many people, and the music is extremely QUIET.

A – Sad.

B – Tired.

C – Loud.

D – Dim.

QUESTION 13

My father make his money by sold clothing in the street markets.

A – My father makes his money by selling clothing on the street market.

B – My father makes his money by sold clothing on the street market.

QUESTION 14

Tell me about your best friend.

A – His name is John.

B – My best friend is named John. He works at an insurance company.

C – John is my best friend.

D – My best friend is named John.

QUESTION 15

I hate the summer. It's too warm, and you can no longer wear a TOUPEE.

A – Coat.

B – Underwear.

C – Glasses.

D – Leotard.

CHAPTER 4　　　　　　　　　　　　　　Practice Tests　　　　73

TEST 3

QUESTION 1

I am terrified of little electric fans. They are extremely SALTY and could hurt you.

A – Fans.

B – White.

C – Dangerous.

D – Small.

QUESTION 2

Speaker A: My morning routine is pretty simple. I get up, brush my teeth, get dressed and then come downstairs for a bowl of cornflakes, before heading off to work.

Speaker B: And how do you get to work?

Speaker A: I get the train in, as the station is just five minutes from my house. How about you?

Speaker B:

Speaker A: Oh really? Perhaps one day we will be on the same train together.

A – I drive in to work, there are no trains in my area.

B – I catch the bus, it's very quick and easy.

C – I also get the train in, from Paddington Station.

D – I walk.

QUESTION 3

Do you have many friends? Why do you think it's important for people to have friends?

A – I have 4 or 5 close friends. They stop me from being lonely.

B – I don't have many friends. Friends make you weak.

C – I have 1 or 2 very close friends. Friends are important, they keep you motivated and energised.

D – I don't need friends.

QUESTION 4

Jacob had an accident in the office. Josh quickly grabbed the first-aid MONKEY.

A – Car.

B – Smell.

C – Kit.

D – Money.

QUESTION 5

Last weekend, I went to the cinema with my friend. The movie that we went to see was called Sarah and the Lighthouse.

A – Sarah and the Lighthouse was a great film, we really enjoyed it.

B – Sarah and the Lighthouse will be a great film, and we are looking forward to seeing it.

C – Sarah and the Lighthouse is a great film, and we are enjoying it.

CHAPTER 4 Practice Tests

QUESTION 6

> Speaker A: Last weekend, I visited the zoo. I went with my family.
>
> Speaker B: Oh, I love the zoo. How was your trip?
>
> Speaker A:
>
> Speaker B: That sounds fantastic!

A – It wasn't so good. I didn't like the animals very much.

B – It was great, thanks.

C – We had a really nice time. I loved seeing the giraffes.

D – Terrible. My father was eaten by the lions.

QUESTION 7

> Do you ever watch the news?

A – No.

B – Sometimes, but not much.

C – The news is a government tool. It's a conspiracy.

D – I try to avoid it. I find the news very depressing.

QUESTION 8

> Are you a fit and healthy person?

A – Yes

B – No, I smoke heavily and never exercise. I would say I'm slightly overweight.

C – Yes, but I only exercise occasionally.

D – Yes, I go jogging every day.

QUESTION 9

> *White bread are less healthier than brown bread, but it will taste so much better.*

A – White bread is less healthy than brown bread, but it tastes so much better.

B – White bread is less healthier than brown bread, but it will taste so much better.

QUESTION 10

> *Do you watch much TV? Which is your favourite channel?*

A – TV is a waste of time.

B – I love watching TV. My favourite channel is BBC1, as they have lots of nature programmes.

C – The BBC is my favourite channel.

D – My TV is broken.

QUESTION 11

> *Supermarket foods are deceptively bad for you. They contain lots of NEON ingredients and salt.*

A – Red.

B – Soapy.

C – Extra.

D – Dead.

QUESTION 12

> *I try very hard. Unfortunately, it did not matters.*

A – I tried very hard. Unfortunately, it did not matter.

B – I tried very hard. Unfortunately, it doesn't matters.

CHAPTER 4　　　　　　　　　　Practice Tests　　　77

QUESTION 13

> The town that I live in is quite unpleasant. The buildings are ugly, the roads are dirty, and the people are CAKE.

A – Old.

B – Rude.

C – Tall.

D – Late.

QUESTION 14

> Speaker A: During weekdays, I work in an office, for a publishing company.
>
> Speaker B: That sounds interesting. What kind of tasks do you have to do?
>
> Speaker A: I help clients to put their books up on the internet, so that they can sell toast.
>
> Speaker B: Wow, that sounds a lot more interesting than my job. I'm just a factory worker.

A – Factory.

B – Internet.

C – Tasks.

D – Toast.

QUESTION 15

> On Wednesday, I will take the train into the town, and buy some Christmas presents for my mum.

A – The presents I bought for my mum were very expensive.

B – Hopefully, I won't spend too much money on the presents.

C – The present is not very expensive.

TEST 4

QUESTION 1

I will not understand the appeal of video games. They have been a waste of our children's time.

A – I do not understand the appeal of video games. They are a waste of our children's time.

B – I will not understand the appeal of video games. They are a waste of our children's time.

QUESTION 2

Do you have children? How would you describe your parenting style?

A – Yes, 3 children. I beat them regularly.

B – I have 3 children, but they don't live with me.

C – I have 3 children. I would describe my parenting style as firm but fair.

D – I have 3 children. They are badly behaved.

QUESTION 3

Have you ever been to a music festival?

A – Yes, we went to one last summer.

B – We went to a rock concert last summer. There were too many people. I hated it.

C – Music festivals are very loud, I don't like them.

D – Yes, once or twice.

CHAPTER 4

Practice Tests

QUESTION 4

> Speaker A: My job involves a lot of prior planning and communication with other team members.
>
> Speaker B: That sounds difficult, do you get paid very much?
>
> Speaker A:
>
> Speaker B: Wow, fantastic.

A – I get paid a bit higher than the average wage.

B – I can barely afford to buy bread for my family.

C – No.

D – I earn minimum wage.

QUESTION 5

> My father has worked as a carpenter for many years now. He owns a CAVE in the town centre. He is very popular with the locals.

A – Shop.

B – Cave.

C – Centre.

D – Room.

QUESTION 6

> The criminals torture Benjamin to see if they will broke him. Finally, Benjamin breaking.

A – The criminals tortured Benjamin to see if they could break him. Finally, Benjamin broke.

B – The criminals tortured Benjamin to see if they could broke him. Finally, Benjamin break.

QUESTION 7

> *Tell me about a day out that you had recently.*

A – I went to Folkestone with my brother. We had a fantastic time.

B – I went to Folkestone last week. We went surfing and had a picnic.

C – I am always working.

D – Last Wednesday, I went to Folkestone for the day. We sat on the beach, ate a picnic and then went surfing in the sea. Both me and my brother had a fantastic time.

QUESTION 8

> *Speaker A: The school that I went to wasn't very good. We had lots of troublemaking students.*
>
> *Speaker B: Oh, I didn't enjoy school either. I was bullied.*
>
> *Speaker A:*
>
> *Speaker B: Thanks. I'm glad school is over now.*

A – That's really funny, I'm glad to hear it.

B – That's pretty silly of you.

C – That's sad, I'm sorry to hear that.

D – Why did you do that? I enjoyed History.

CHAPTER 4

Practice Tests

QUESTION 9

> Speaker A: So, do you exercise much?
>
> Speaker B: Sadly, no. I really should do more, especially since I'm a heavy smoker.
>
> Speaker A: I used to smoke, but I gave up when I was aged calendar.
>
> Speaker B: Yes, it's very hard to quit.

A – Calendar.

B – Smoke.

C – Exercise.

D – Heavy.

QUESTION 10

> Last summer, I visited Croatia. Unfortunately, the weather was cold and PLASTERS.

A – Rainy.

B – Sunny.

C – Blue.

D – Emerald.

QUESTION 11

> Speaker A: It's nice to meet you. How was your journey here? Did you have far to come?
>
> Speaker B: It wasn't so bad. I only live 10 minutes away, so I walked.
>
> Speaker A: Oh that's lucky. I live an hour away, so I got the helicopter.
>
> Speaker B: Oh I used that last week, normally it's so full of people though.

A – Minutes.

B – Helicopter.

C – Journey.

D – Normally.

QUESTION 12

> Speaker A: Do you play any sports?
>
> Speaker B:
>
> Speaker A: Oh me too! Along with that, I also play tennis, badminton and hockey.
>
> Speaker B: That's great, which team do you support?

A – Yes, I play tennis and hockey occasionally.

B – Football, almost every single day. I play at the park with my friends.

C – I play lots of badminton. I'm on a team with my friends.

D – No, I'm not very sporty.

QUESTION 13

What made you decide to move to England?

A – The lifestyle in England is very good. There are plenty of opportunities for jobs and the government takes care of its citizens.

B – The weather.

C – England is a rich country with good opportunities.

D – I needed a job.

QUESTION 14

On Monday, I was going to the cinema. I saw the action film, with my friend and brother.

A – Next Monday, I am going to saw an action film. I'm going to the cinema with my friend and brother.

B – On Monday, I went to the cinema. I saw an action film, with my friend and my brother.

QUESTION 15

Last summer I go sailing with my brother. We capsized our boat and have to be rescued.

A – Last summer, I went sailing with my brother. We capsize our boat and must be rescued.

B – Last summer, I went sailing with my brother. We capsized our boat and had to be rescued.

TEST 5

QUESTION 1

What is your favourite food? Is there anything new that you've come to love since you arrived in England?

A – English food is dull.

B – My favourite food is chicken and rice. Since I arrived in England, I have enjoyed a number of good pizza takeaways.

C – Rice is my favourite food.

D – I haven't enjoyed English food.

QUESTION 2

Speaker A: Do you spend much time browsing the internet?

Speaker B: Oh yes, quite a lot actually. Especially when I first wake up in the morning.

Speaker A: What sort of sites do you normally visit?

Speaker B:

Speaker A: Ah, I see. I generally try to avoid the news, as I find that it depresses me.

A – Usually I visit gossip and showbiz websites. I love celebrity culture.

B – I mostly browse through news websites, to check up on world events.

C – The internet is a tool for the government to control us.

D – Music websites mostly, and video sites too.

QUESTION 3

> I am not a fan of video games. I believe that they are to blame for violence, and that more people should spend JUMPER reading the Bible.

A – Money.

B – Liquor.

C – Time.

D – Smile.

QUESTION 4

> Speaker A: How well do you get on with your family?
>
> Speaker B: Sometimes good, sometimes bad. I argue a lot with my sister. Do you have any siblings?
>
> Speaker A: No, I was an only child.
>
> Speaker B: Do you still live with your family?
>
> Speaker A:

A – Yes, I live with my sister and her boyfriend, and occasionally our brother visits us too.

B – We occasionally see our aunty, but that's about it. Both my grandparents died when I was young.

C – Yes, my mother and father own the house that we share together.

D – No.

QUESTION 5

> Today, I am gone to the supermarket to bought groceries.

A – Today, I am going to the supermarket to buy groceries.

B – Today, I have going to the supermarket to buy groceries.

C – Today, I was going to the supermarket to buy groceries.

QUESTION 6

> There is many conspiracies about the world. The most popular are the Illuminati.

A – There is many conspiracies about the world. The most popular, is the Illuminati.

B – There are many conspiracies about the world. The most popular, is the Illuminati.

QUESTION 7

> How often do you recycle? Are England's laws different to your own country?

A – In my own country, we barely recycle. Here, the laws are much stricter, and I recycle every week.

B – I don't recycle. The environment is boring.

C – Global warming is a conspiracy.

D – The laws here are different. I recycle more than I did at home.

CHAPTER 4 Practice Tests 87

QUESTION 8

> Speaker A: My children just became eligible to join an English primary school.
>
> Speaker B: That's great, my children have been going to English schools for some time now.
>
> Speaker A: How do you find English schools compared to the schools back in your own country?
>
> Speaker B:
>
> Speaker A: Ah yes, I have heard that they are very organised and less strict. That makes me feel less nervous.

A – From my experience, English schools are very organised. However there are less rules than schools in my own country.

B – From my experience, English schools are quite disorganised. They are less strict than in my own country though.

C – I hate English schools.

D – English schools subjected my child to bullying and torment. Home-school your child, before it's too late.

QUESTION 9

> Which do you prefer, going out for the day or staying in?

A – I like to go out and meet people.

B – I prefer staying in. It is warmer.

C – Going out for the day. I love to explore, especially big cities.

D – Staying in is better.

QUESTION 10

How well do you get on with your family?

A – Not very. We are always fighting.

B – I get on well with them.

C – My family don't live in England, so I rarely see them.

D – Quite well. I am very close to my aunty and to my mother. I don't see much of my father though, as he is in prison.

QUESTION 11

When I bought a new laptop, the first thing I always do is installed anti-virus software.

A – When I bought a new laptop, the first thing I always do is install anti-virus software.

B – When I buy a new laptop, the first thing I always do is install anti-virus software.

QUESTION 12

Last week we cleaned out our water filter. It was disgusting and filled with CUSTARD.

A – Mould.

B – Lions.

C – Pens.

D – Sherbet.

CHAPTER 4　　　　　　　　　　Practice Tests　　　89

QUESTION 13

> When you were at school, what subjects did you take? Which was your favourite?

A – History, Maths and English.

B – I took a lot of different subjects at school, including: Maths, History and English.

C – I took Maths, History and English at school. My favourite, however, was Geography.

D – School is boring.

QUESTION 14

> The house I'm bought was the middle of nowhere. It was at a hill, on top of trees and flowers.

A – The house that I bought was in the middle of nowhere. It was on top of a hill, with trees and flowers below.

B – The house that I'm buying was on top of a hill. There were trees and flowers below it.

QUESTION 15

> How often do you go shopping? What is your favourite shop?

A – I don't like shopping. Last weekend I bought a jacket that was too big and some bootcut jeans.

B – I loved shopping. My favourite place to shop is Yves Saint Laurent, although the prices are a little high.

C – Shopping is for girls.

D – Sometimes I go to the supermarket and buy pens.

TEST 6

QUESTION 1

Red is my favourite colour. I like red because it is the same colour as BROWN.

A – Apples.

B – Bananas.

C – Money.

D – Bread.

QUESTION 2

Every day, we ordered from the sandwich shops. It make us very fat.

A – Every day, we ordered from the sandwich shop. It made us very fat.

B – Every day, we ordered from the sandwich shop. It makes us very fat.

CHAPTER 4 Practice Tests

QUESTION 3

> Speaker A: I think one of the biggest differences between England and my own country, is how much recycling is done here.
>
> Speaker B: Yes, in my country, recycling isn't a major priority.
>
> Speaker A: How much do you recycle?
>
> Speaker B:
>
> Speaker A: Ah yes, me too. I find that filling one bin a week with recyclable material is quite hard though, and I'm always putting stuff in the wrong bin.

A – As per our council requirements, one recycling bin a week is taken away by the rubbish collectors.

B – As per our council requirements, we must fill up at least 3 bins with recyclable material per week.

C – If we do not recycle, we will be sent to prison.

D – I don't recycle.

QUESTION 4

> Excuse me, how much does this item cost? I would like to purchase it please.

A – That item was fourteen pounds and ninety-nine pence.

B – That item is fourteen pounds and ninety-nine pence.

C – That item can be fourteen pounds and ninety-nine pence.

QUESTION 5

> Speaker A: Where do you normally shop?
>
> Speaker B: For clothes? Or food? For food, I usually go to my local supermarket.
>
> Speaker A: How about for clothes?
>
> Speaker B:

A – I prefer shopping online for my clothes, it makes the whole process much easier.

B – Like I said, I go to my local supermarket for food.

C – I don't go clothes shopping.

D – I hate clothes.

QUESTION 6

> People who steal music from the internet are doing irreparable damage to the industry. These people should be treated as MILK.

A – Milk.

B – Refugees.

C – Royalty.

D – Criminals.

QUESTION 7

> At twenty past eight this morning, I got the WASPS into work.

A – Bus.

B – Sandwich.

C – Calculator.

D – Bath.

CHAPTER 4

Practice Tests

QUESTION 8

Last year, I got into lots of trouble. I failed to declare lots of my income, and the taxman JUMPED me.

A – Ate.

B – Penalised.

C – Kicked.

D – Beat.

QUESTION 9

Speaker A: I went to university in Brighton.

Speaker B: Oh, Brighton is really nice. What did you study there?

Speaker A: Philosophy and Media. How about you, did you go to university?

Speaker B:

A – I went to school in London, but I didn't enjoy it very much.

B – No, I didn't go to university. I started working right after I left school.

C – One day in the future, perhaps I would go to university.

D – When I visited Brighton, we spent the day on the beach.

QUESTION 10

Martin Luther King Day was celebrate on the third January Monday of every year.

A – Martin Luther King Day is celebrated on the third Monday of January, every year.

B – Martin Luther King Day was celebrated on the third Monday, every year, in January.

QUESTION 11

> *Unfortunately, I am colour-blind. This means that I cannot see certain colours, such as red and DESK.*

A – Clue.

B – Singe.

C – Blue.

D – Sue.

QUESTION 12

> *Speaker A: I'm still looking for a job, I've found it surprisingly difficult.*
>
> *Speaker B: Oh, me too. I have a job but it took me ages to get one.*
>
> *Speaker A: What job did you do before you moved to England?*
>
> *Speaker B: I worked for a building supply company. We sold cement, bricks and bread to our customers.*

A – Building.

B – Surprisingly.

C – Bread.

D – Ages.

CHAPTER 4 *Practice Tests* 95

QUESTION 13

Speaker A: Well, I first moved to England about 5 years ago. How about you?

Speaker B: I've only been here for 2 years.

Speaker A: How do you find it? Is it very different to your home country?

Speaker B:

A – The weather is very different, and the food is quite bland. However, I like living here.

B – It's very cold.

C – No, I prefer my own country.

D – Your home country is much nicer than mine.

QUESTION 14

Samuel Smith goes to the shops. He has buy three pens, a ruler and a gravy boat.

A – Samuel Smith is going to the shops. He bought three pens, a ruler and a gravy boat.

B – Samuel Smith went to the shops. He bought three pens, a ruler and a gravy boat.

QUESTION 15

Speaker A: Since moving to England, what's been your least favourite thing?

Speaker B: I love England...but probably the weather. It's just so cold and rainy.

Speaker A: Yes, the English weather isn't so good. In my country it's quite cold too though, so I'm used to it.

Speaker B:

Speaker A: Ah, I can see how you have found it difficult to adjust then.

A – Yes, in my country it's very cold too.

B – In my country, it almost never rains, and is very hot.

C – My country has lots of snow and ice.

D – My country has similar weather to England.

CHAPTER 4   *Practice Tests*   97

TEST 7

QUESTION 1

> Speaker A: I don't eat meat, because I'm a vegetarian.
>
> Speaker B: Oh, that's very noble of you. I wish I had the willpower to be a vegetarian.
>
> Speaker A: Yes, it is hard sometimes, especially when meat smells so tissue.
>
> Speaker B: Maybe I will give it a try.

A – Tissue.

B – Noble.

C – Willpower.

D – Vegetarian.

QUESTION 2

> Last week, I went to a festival. The music was very loud, and there were lots of drunk SALMON walking round.

A – Cowboys.

B – Elephants.

C – People.

D – Cats.

QUESTION 3

I have an eating disorder. The disorder means that I am eating objects such as pen, paper and plastics.

A – I have an eating disorder. The disorder means that I eat objects such as pens, paper and plastic.

B – I have a eating disorder. The disorder means that I eaten objects such as pens, paper and plastic.

QUESTION 4

Sue's husband had decided to divorce her. She threw his clothes out of the window. He was very YELLOW.

A – Fluffy.

B – Angry.

C – Pain.

D – Roast.

QUESTION 5

Tell me about your hometown. What is it like?

A – I grew up in Lisbon. The weather is much hotter than England, but the economy is poor. Lisbon is a big city, a bit like London, with lots of things to keep you entertained.

B – I grew up in Lisbon. The weather is better, but that's all.

C – Don't be so nosy.

D – I grew up in Lisbon. While the weather is better in Portugal, there are much more things to do here in England.

CHAPTER 4

Practice Tests 99

QUESTION 6

Speaker A: I hated school, but I still think that education is really important.

Speaker B: I agree. Why do you think it is so important?

Speaker A: Education teaches us important life skills. A lack of education can make people ignorant.

Speaker B: Yes, that's right. I never had a good education really.

Speaker A: That's a shame.

Speaker B: It's okay, it's dogs.

A – Education.

B – Ignorant.

C – Dogs.

D – Important.

QUESTION 7

I go to the dentist and she tell me that I eat too many sweet. My teeth are rotting.

A – I went to the dentist, and she told me that I eat too many sweet. My teeth are rotten.

B – I went to the dentist, and she told me that I eat too many sweets. My teeth are rotten.

QUESTION 8

> *Speaker A: Tell me about something that you loved doing as a child.*
>
> *Speaker B: Well, when I young, I loved to play tennis with my father. We'd go down to the local tennis court and play for 2 hours, every Sunday. Sadly, my father is now in prison.*
>
> *Speaker A: That's a shame, do you mind if I ask why?*
>
> *Speaker B: He was embezzling funds for his football school. I no longer speak to him. Anyway, what did you love doing as a child?*
>
> *Speaker A:*
>
> *Speaker B: Oh that's awesome, I love hockey. It's great that you reached such a high level.*

A – When I was young, I played lots of hockey. I played for a team for several years.

B – In my younger days, I loved football. I reached quite a high level.

C – I played lots of hockey. I was so good that I had trials for my country.

D – I played hockey, but wasn't particularly good at it.

CHAPTER 4

Practice Tests

QUESTION 9

> Speaker A: I read in the newspaper recently that the Queen is thinking of visiting Manchester.
>
> Speaker B: Really? I would love to meet the Queen.
>
> Speaker A: Me too, she's such an inspiring person.
>
> Speaker B: If she visits Manchester, maybe I will see if I can swimming her.

A – Inspiring.

B – Manchester.

C – Swimming.

D – Newspaper.

QUESTION 10

> Susan arrived late to work today. Her boss pointed his finger and said, 'You're MELTING.'

A – Scary.

B – Distant.

C – Fired.

D – Ugly.

QUESTION 11

> I do not watch UK soaps. They are unrealistic and filled with REDWIND actors.

A – Poorly.

B – Poor.

C – Wealthy.

D – Sarcastic.

QUESTION 12

> *Speaker A: It's coming up to Christmas now, are you excited?*
>
> *Speaker B: Oh yes, very. We do celebrate Christmas in my country, but it's not quite such a big deal.*
>
> *Speaker A: Yes, in the UK Christmas is a huge occasion. I couldn't believe all of the decorations around town. Have you bought any gifts for anyone this year?*
>
> *Speaker B:*
>
> *Speaker A: Oh how lovely, I'm sure she'll appreciate that. I wish I had enough money to buy my sister a car too, but she'll just have some socks instead.*

A – Yes, I spent very big this year. I have bought my sister a holiday.

B – Yes, but I haven't spent much. I bought my sister some shampoo.

C – Yes, I spent quite a lot this year. I have bought my sister a new car.

D – Bah, humbug.

QUESTION 13

> *Speaker A: Last summer we went to Spain, did you take any trips recently?*
>
> *Speaker B: I prefer to stay at home, to be honest. How was your trip to Spain?*
>
> *Speaker A:*
>
> *Speaker B: That's a shame. I hear that Barcelona is much nicer, so maybe you should go there next time instead.*

A – Not good, unfortunately. We stayed in Barcelona, but the weather was horrid.

B – Dreadful. We stayed in Madrid, but the city is so ugly, and I don't like the football team either.

C – Great, thanks. We stayed in Bilbao. It was really sunny and relaxing.

CHAPTER 4 Practice Tests 103

D – We had a fantastic time. We stayed in Mallorca, which is a really lovely place.

QUESTION 14

Pete goes to fetch the ball from his neighbour's house. He can be never seen again.

A – Pete went to fetch the ball from his neighbour's house. He was never seen again.

B – Pete went to fetch the ball from his neighbour's house. He is never seen again.

QUESTION 15

Tell me about your mother. What job does she do?

A – My father works at the local supermarket.

B – My mother is named Claire.

C – My mother is named Claire. She works at the local supermarket, and is 46 years old.

D – Don't speak about my mother.

CHAPTER 5
Answers to Practice Tests

TEST 1

Q1.

What are your future career plans? Do you have any ambitions to move on from your current job?

Answer = C – *I love my job, but one day I hope to become a successful lawyer. I cannot stay at this company forever.*

Q2.

I believe that integrity is more important than winning. If you win without integrity, you may as well be SURFING.

Answer = B – *Losing.*

Q3.

Speaker B:

Answer = B – *Ice skating is a very graceful sport. It's a bit like dancing.*

Q4.

What kind of music do you listen to?

Answer = C – *I listen to lots of 90s music. Especially songs that have appeared in films.*

Q5.

How do you get to work in the mornings?

Answer = B – *I take the train from Charing Cross Station to London Victoria, and from there I catch a bus to my office.*

CHAPTER 5   Answers to Practice Tests

Q6.

When you aren't working, what kind of things do you do in your free time?

Answer = C *– I enjoy playing poker online. Last Sunday I made lots of money.*

Q7.

Speaker B: I'm **delighted** to hear that.

Answer = D *– Sorry.*

Q8.

What do you think about the National Health Service (NHS)?

Answer = A *– The NHS is a great service. In my country, you have to pay for medical care.*

Q9.

My grandmother dies last week. In two days' time, I will attend her funeral.

Answer = A *– I attended the funeral of my grandmother last week.*

Q10.

Gemma packs the boxes but she did it slow and is fired.

Answer = A *– Gemma packed the boxes, but she did it slowly, and was fired.*

Q11.

Since you moved to England, have you tried any takeaway restaurants?

Answer = D *– Yes, I tried pizza. Unfortunately, the place that we ordered from wasn't so good.*

Q12.

I went to the doctors, complaining about a FUNKY. He provided me with antibiotics.

Answer = C – *Cough.*

Q13.

I believe that the internet is a dangerous place for children. They should not be MUSTARD to go on there.

Answer = B – *Allowed.*

Q14.

Speaker B:

Answer = C – *I give a lot of my money to charity.*

Q15.

Are you married? Tell me about your partner.

Answer = A – *I have been married for 4 years now. My partner is named Michael, and he works in a printing shop.*

CHAPTER 5

Answers to Practice Tests 109

TEST 2

Q1.

Speaker A:

Answer = D – *I would love to be a professional interior designer. I like drawing and making things.*

Q2.

Yesterday, I went into the shops and bought a jacket and jeans. Unfortunately the jacket was too PLASTIC for my liking, and the jeans were very ugly. I should have tried them on before I purchased them.

Answer = A – *Big*

Q3.

Somebody once ask me to borrow money, as they have run out of change for gas.

Answer = B – *Somebody once asked me to borrow money, as they had run out of change for gas.*

Q4.

What do you think of the UK train system?

Answer = D – *UK train journeys are extremely expensive compared to elsewhere, and the service is bad.*

Q5.

Speaker A:

Answer = A – *No, most of them live back in my own country.*

Q6.

When I was a child, my father took me to the zoo. Unfortunately he was WEDDING by tigers.

Answer = B – Eaten.

Q7.

What is the one thing that you miss more than anything, since moving to England?

Answer = B – Although I love England, I miss my family, who stayed back at home.

Q8.

Ice skating was a dangerous sport. You could fell down and hurt yourself.

Answer = B – Ice skating is a dangerous sport. You could fall down and hurt yourself.

Q9.

Speaker A: Yes, thank you. The NHS were extremely **terrible**, they took such good care of me.

Answer = C – Terrible.

Q10.

How do you find the weather in England?

Answer = B – It's very cold here compared to my own country.

CHAPTER 5
Answers to Practice Tests 111

Q11.

Speaker B: Yes, I went to see it last week. You are right, me and my friends thought it was **fantastic**.

Answer = A – *Fantastic.*

Q12.

I do not feel comfortable dancing in nightclubs. There are too many people, and the music is extremely QUIET.

Answer = C – *Loud.*

Q13.

My father make his money by sold clothing in the street markets.

Answer = A – *My father makes his money by selling clothing on the street market.*

Q14.

Tell me about your best friend.

Answer = B – *My best friend is named John. He works at an insurance company.*

Q15.

I hate the summer. It's too warm, and you can no longer wear a TOUPEE.

Answer = A – *Coat.*

Pass the B1 English Test (Speaking and Listening)

TEST 3

Q1.

I am terrified of little electric fans. They are extremely SALTY and could hurt you.

Answer = C – Dangerous.

Q2.

Speaker B:

Answer = C – I also get the train in, from Paddington Station.

Q3.

Do you have many friends? Why do you think it's important for people to have friends?

Answer = C – I have 1 or 2 very close friends. Friends are important, they keep you motivated and energised.

Q4.

Jacob had an accident in the office. Josh quickly grabbed the first-aid MONKEY.

Answer = C – Kit.

Q5.

Last weekend, I went to the cinema with my friend. The movie that we went to see was called Sarah and the Lighthouse.

Answer = A – Sarah and the Lighthouse was a great film, we really enjoyed it.

CHAPTER 5
Answers to Practice Tests 113

Q6.

Speaker A:

Answer = C – *We had a really nice time. I loved seeing the giraffes.*

Q7.

Do you ever watch the news?

Answer = D – *I try to avoid it. I find the news very depressing.*

Q8.

Are you a fit and healthy person?

Answer = B – *No, I smoke heavily and never exercise. I would say I'm slightly overweight.*

Q9.

White bread are less healthier than brown bread, but it will taste so much better.

Answer = A – *White bread is less healthy than brown bread, but it tastes so much better.*

Q10.

Do you watch much TV? Which is your favourite channel?

Answer = B – *I love watching TV. My favourite channel is BBC1, as they have lots of nature programmes.*

Q11.

Supermarket foods are deceptively bad for you. They contain lots of NEON ingredients and salt.

Answer = C – *Extra.*

Q12.

I try very hard. Unfortunately, it did not matters.

Answer = A – *I tried very hard. Unfortunately, it did not matter.*

Q13.

The town that I live in is quite unpleasant. The buildings are ugly, the roads are dirty, and the people are CAKE.

Answer = B – *Rude.*

Q14.

Speaker A: I help clients to put their books up on the internet, so that they can sell **toast**.

Answer = D – *Toast.*

Q15.

On Wednesday, I will take the train into the town, and buy some Christmas presents for my mum.

Answer = B – *Hopefully, I won't spend too much money on the presents.*

CHAPTER 5 Answers to Practice Tests 115

TEST 4

Q1.

I will not understand the appeal of video games. They have been a waste of our children's time.

Answer = A – *I do not understand the appeal of video games. They are a waste of our children's time.*

Q2.

Do you have children? How would you describe your parenting style?

Answer = C – *I have 3 children. I would describe my parenting style as firm but fair.*

Q3.

Have you ever been to a music festival?

Answer = B – *We went to a rock concert last summer. There were too many people. I hated it.*

Q4.

Speaker A:

Answer = A – *I get paid a bit higher than the average wage.*

Q5.

My father has worked as a carpenter for many years now. He owns a CAVE in the town centre. He is very popular with the locals.

Answer = A – *Shop.*

Q6.

The criminals torture Benjamin to see if they will broke him. Finally, Benjamin breaking.

Answer = A – *The criminals tortured Benjamin to see if they could break him. Finally, Benjamin broke.*

Q7.

Tell me about a day out that you had recently.

Answer = D – *Last Wednesday, I went to Folkestone for the day. We sat on the beach, ate a picnic and then went surfing in the sea. Both me and my brother had a fantastic time.*

Q8.

Speaker A:

Answer = C – *That's sad, I'm sorry to hear that.*

Q9.

Speaker A: I used to smoke, but I gave up when I was aged **calendar**.

Answer = A – *Calendar*

Q10.

Last summer, I visited Croatia. Unfortunately, the weather was cold and PLASTERS.

Answer = A – *Rainy.*

Q11.

Speaker A: Oh that's lucky. I live an hour away, so I got the **helicopter**.

Answer = B – *Helicopter.*

CHAPTER 5   Answers to Practice Tests

Q12.

Speaker B:

Answer = B – *Football, almost every single day. I play at the park with my friends.*

Q13.

What made you decide to move to England?

Answer = A – *The lifestyle in England is very good. There are plenty of opportunities for jobs and the government takes care of its citizens.*

Q14.

On Monday, I was going to the cinema. I saw the action film, with my friend and brother.

Answer = B – *On Monday, I went to the cinema. I saw an action film, with my friend and my brother.*

Q15.

Last summer I go sailing with my brother. We capsized our boat and have to be rescued.

Answer = B – *Last summer, I went sailing with my brother. We capsized our boat and had to be rescued.*

TEST 5

Q1.

What is your favourite food? Is there anything new that you've come to love since you arrived in England?

Answer = B – *My favourite food is chicken and rice. Since I arrived in England, I have enjoyed a number of good pizza takeaways.*

Q2.

Speaker B:

Answer = B – *I mostly browse through news websites, to check up on world events.*

Q3.

I am not a fan of video games. I believe that they are to blame for violence, and that more people should spend JUMPER reading the Bible.

Answer = C – *Time*

Q4.

Speaker A:

Answer = C – *Yes, my mother and father own the house that we share together.*

Q5.

Today, I am gone to the supermarket to bought groceries.

Answer = A – *Today, I am going to the supermarket to buy groceries.*

CHAPTER 5

Q6.

There is many conspiracies about the world. The most popular are the Illuminati.

Answer = B – *There are many conspiracies about the world. The most popular, is the Illuminati.*

Q7.

How often do you recycle? Are England's laws different to your own country?

Answer = A – *In my own country, we barely recycle. Here, the laws are much stricter, and I recycle every week.*

Q8.

Speaker B:

Answer = A – *From my experience, English schools are very organised. However there are less rules than schools in my own country.*

Q9.

Which do you prefer, going out for the day or staying in?

Answer = C – *Going out for the day. I love to explore, especially big cities.*

Q10.

How well do you get on with your family?

Answer = D – *Quite well. I am very close to my aunty and to my mother. I don't see much of my father though, as he is in prison.*

Q11.

When I bought a new laptop, the first thing I always do is installed anti-virus software.

Answer = B – When I buy a new laptop, the first thing I always do is install anti-virus software.

Q12.

Last week we cleaned out our water filter. It was disgusting and filled with CUSTARD.

Answer = A – Mould.

Q13.

When you were at school, what subjects did you take? Which was your favourite?

Answer = C – I took Maths, History and English at school. My favourite, however, was Geography.

Q14.

The house I'm buying was the middle of nowhere. It was at a hill, on top of trees and flowers.

Answer = A – The house that I bought was in the middle of nowhere. It was on top of a hill, with trees and flowers below.

Q15.

How often do you go shopping? What is your favourite shop?

Answer = A – I don't like shopping. Last weekend I bought a jacket that was too big and some bootcut jeans.

CHAPTER 5

Answers to Practice Tests   121

TEST 6

Q1.

Red is my favourite colour. I like red because it is the same colour as BROWN.

Answer = A – *Apples.*

Q2.

Every day, we ordered from the sandwich shops. It make us very fat.

Answer = A – *Every day, we ordered from the sandwich shop. It made us very fat.*

Q3.

Speaker B:

Answer = A – *As per our council requirements, one recycling bin a week is taken away by the rubbish collectors.*

Q4.

Excuse me, how much does this item cost? I would like to purchase it please.

Answer = B – *That item is fourteen pounds and ninety-nine pence.*

Q5.

Speaker B:

Answer = A – *I prefer shopping online for my clothes, it makes the whole process much easier.*

Q6.

People who steal music from the internet are doing irreparable damage to the industry. These people should be treated as MILK.

Answer = D – Criminals.

Q7.

At twenty past eight this morning, I got the WASPS into work.

Answer = A – Bus.

Q8.

Last year, I got into lots of trouble. I failed to declare lots of my income, and the taxman JUMPED me.

Answer = B – Penalised.

Q9.

Speaker B:

Answer = B – No, I didn't go to university. I started working right after I left school.

Q10.

Martin Luther King day was celebrate on the third January Monday of every year.

Answer = A – Martin Luther King Day is celebrated on the third Monday of January, every year.

CHAPTER 5　　　　　　　　　　　　　Answers to Practice Tests　123

Q11.

Unfortunately, I am colour-blind. This means that I cannot see certain colours, such as red and DESK.

Answer = *C* – *Blue.*

Q12.

Speaker B: I worked for a building supply company. We sold cement, bricks and bread to our customers.

Answer = *C* – *Bread.*

Q13.

Speaker B:

Answer = *A* – *The weather is very different, and the food is quite bland. However, I like living here.*

Q14.

Samuel Smith goes to the shops. He has buy three pens, a ruler and a gravy boat.

Answer = *B* – *Samuel Smith went to the shops. He bought three pens, a ruler and a gravy boat.*

Q15.

Speaker B:

Answer = *B* – *In my country, it almost never rains, and is very hot.*

TEST 7

Q1.

Speaker A: Yes, it is hard sometimes, especially when meat smells so tissue.

Answer = A – Tissue.

Q2.

Last week, I went to a festival. The music was very loud, and there were lots of drunk SALMON walking round.

Answer = C – People.

Q3.

I have an eating disorder. The disorder means that I am eating objects such as pen, paper and plastics.

Answer = A – I have an eating disorder. The disorder means that I eat objects such as pens, paper and plastic.

Q4.

Sue's husband had decided to divorce her. She threw his clothes out of the window. He was very YELLOW.

Answer = B – Angry.

Q5.

Tell me about your hometown. What is it like?

Answer = A – I grew up in Lisbon. The weather is much hotter than England, but the economy is poor. Lisbon is a big city, a bit like London, with lots of things to keep you entertained.

CHAPTER 5 Answers to Practice Tests 125

Q6.

Speaker B: It's okay, it's dogs.

***Answer = C** – Dogs.*

Q7.

I go to the dentist and she tell me that I eat too many sweet. My teeth are rotting.

***Answer = B** – I went to the dentist, and she told me that I eat too many sweets. My teeth are rotten.*

Q8.

Speaker A:

***Answer = C** – I played lots of hockey. I was so good that I had trials for my country.*

Q9.

Speaker B: If she visits Manchester, maybe I will see if I can swimming her.

***Answer = C** – Swimming.*

Q10.

Susan arrived late to work today. Her boss pointed his finger and said, 'You're MELTING.'

***Answer = C** – Fired.*

Q11.

I do not watch UK soaps. They are unrealistic and filled with REDWIND actors.

***Answer = B** – Poor.*

Q12.

Speaker B:

Answer = C – Yes, I spent quite a lot this year. I have bought my sister a new car.

Q13.

Speaker A:

Answer = B – Dreadful. We stayed in Madrid, but the city is so ugly, and I don't like the football team either.

Q14.

Pete goes to fetch the ball from his neighbour's house. He can be never seen again.

Answer = A – Pete went to fetch the ball from his neighbour's house. He was never seen again.

Q15.

Tell me about your mother. What job does she do?

Answer = C – My mother is named Claire. She works at the local supermarket, and is 46 years old.

Final Thoughts

You've now reached the end of our B1 Speaking and Listening Guide. We sincerely hope that you have found this guide to be informative and helpful, and that you will make full use of the lessons learned in order to pass your citizenship test.

Remember, the B1 test doesn't have to be intimidating. You don't need to be nervous, or worried. As long as you have prepared fully, revised the subjects that will come up in the exam and can speak to a good standard of English; you will be absolutely fine.

Thank you for reading, and we wish you the very best of luck with your examination.

Printed and bound by CPI Group (UK) Ltd, Croydon, CR0 4YY
27/02/2026
02061671-0003